JOY & PURPOSE
IN THE FIRST THREE YEARS

SUSAN MAYCLIN STEPHENSON

BOOK #1 OF THE *MONTESSORI FOR FAMILY AND COMMUNITY* SERIES

ADAPTED FROM THE BOOK *MONTESSORI FOR FAMILY AND COMMUNITY*

NOTE: Scan the QR codes in this book
to access short child development videos,
from the author's international work,
that have been uploaded to YouTube

II

CONTENTS

IV

INTRODUCTION

During my 1963-1964 university semester, I took a course on family traditions and religions in various cultures. This research took place in sixteen countries in Europe, the Middle East, and Asia. Since that time, I have continued to search for the best way for human beings to grow and live in over seventy countries and am still learning. Today, discoveries in psychology and neuroscience back up what I have discovered, that the words "joy" and "purpose" are linked in the most successful examples of living life—throughout childhood and adult life. Having a purpose that provides physical, mental, emotional, and spiritual balance in one's own life naturally results in a desire to contribute to the good of all. And a feeling of joy is often the result.

The following pages contain first-hand observation and conclusions that foster understanding of, and support for, optimum development in the first three years of life. This small book is adapted from the first of four sections of the book *Montessori for Family and Community*.

JOY

Even before birth a human being is learning by touching, seeing light and dark, and listening. The newborn has 100 billion neurons and is ready to start strengthening connections, that means he is ready to start learning. His education has begun.

He will learn about love and acceptance by how he is treated, how quickly and gently his needs are met.

He will learn to love and trust himself by how his attempts to develop—physically, mentally, and emotionally—are allowed and supported.

He will begin to learn about the world through experience in the world of the family and close community.

This is joyful learning.

PURPOSE

The purpose of the adult is to observe and support the purpose of the child, which is to fulfil himself.

Observation is a skill used by parents and teachers at all ages and the more an adult learns the more easily an infant's needs can be met. Each cry is a message and adults can learn what is being expressed; is he cold or warm? Is there some discomfort of pressure or wetness? Is he unable to see something interesting? Is movement being impeded?

A Mongolian example, discovering a child's purpose

Sometimes one hears that it takes a lot of money to follow Montessori ideas in the home, but this is not the case. It is the continued learning of us adults—informing our support of his inborn drive to follow a unique path of development—that the child needs.

In 2018 I was in Mongolia to share Montessori ideas and to learn more about the child-raising traditions of this country. My hosts and I traveled far into the countryside to find a traditional family situation with young children. We found a family with two children living in a *ger*, or *yurt*, that was packed up and moved several times during the grazing season to follow the herd's need for fresh grass. The ger consisted of two beds, a table, a cooking/heating stove in the middle, an altar, and a few storage units for clothing, etc.

As the father was out with the animals we talked to the mother, a well-educated high school physics teacher who, along with her husband, chose to spend the summer months caring for family's herds of horses and yaks. She understood the value of a good education but, like many other people, thought that education begins around age six or seven years. Their plan was to move to the city when the children were old enough to attend school.

I wanted to learn about Mongolian practices, but soon we were into deep discussion about the first year of life, about the need for free-movement, and language, and how meeting these needs is not dependent on material objects, but on the knowledge, and observation skills, of the adult.

The four-month-old baby was tied to the wall of the tiny home so he wouldn't fall off onto the floor. He had been given a piece of dried yak cheese to chew on, an excellent tradition that strengthens the jaws and supports the even spacing of teeth later.

As we were speaking, I noticed the great effort the infant was making as he reached for and handled the cheese, and I suggested that we watch carefully to see what was going on. At times he held the cheese in his mouth and tasted it. Sometimes it fell to just out of his reach. At these times he used his whole body to reach and grasp it. His face was serious and determined; his wrist and fingers working hard; his whole body was rocking side to side to try to aid the reach.

I explained that this was just one example of extremely valuable developmental "work" and already an important educational experience. Neuroscientists tell us what is happening in the brain when the mind and the body work together to reach a goal: new pathways in the brain are being formed; skills are being improved; intelligence is improving. And very importantly, the young child is learning to trust himself, and to focus deeply. Because she was a scientist, this mother understood, and our discussion became very interesting.

Traditions?

We began to discuss traditions. There is great wisdom to be had by listening to elders in any community. However, sometimes there is a practice, a tradition, that was valuable in one situation, but not always.

Swaddling, or wrapping a baby so securely that he is unable to move, is one of these traditions. I have spoken to friends who were swaddled when they were young during the Soviet Union era because during that time every adult was required to work every day, all day. There was no one available to watch over very young children, so there was very little free-movement, and more time sleeping, adults could get their work done. Swaddling was their solution.

As this mother showed us the tradition of swaddling it was very clear to all of us that this young boy had more important things to do, and he was very angry at being interrupted from his work!

I told her that even back in the USA today, some parents sometimes thinking swaddling is good for their babies, but more sleeping and less movement is not good for babies.

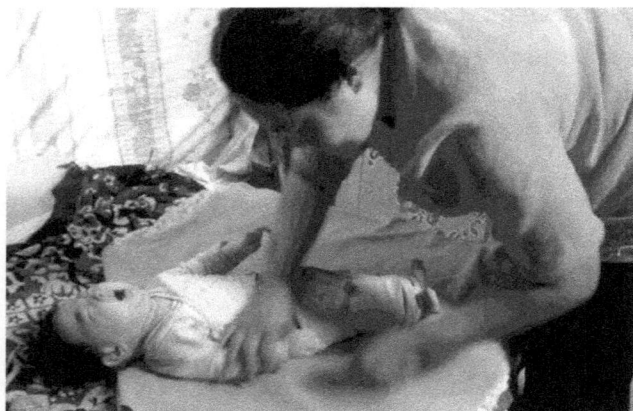

SLEEPING

Montessori parents and teachers are aware that the human has inborn wisdom that tells one when to go to sleep, when to wake up, what to eat, how much, what kind of movement is valuable right now, and on and on.

It is a mistake to thinking of *putting a child to sleep*—sometimes by swaddling and sometimes by nursing, or rocking, or even going for a ride in a car—when the best practice is to support the child in learning to put himself to sleep, and to wake up, following inner wisdom.

Here is a supportive quote from a Montessori teacher, mother, grandmother, head of school, from the book *The Joyful Child: Montessori, Global Wisdom for Birth to Three* (which has been translated into Mongolian partly because of this meeting):

Please do not make our mistake of nursing Claire to sleep at night. In the uterus she had had lots of practice waking and going to sleep according to her mental and physical needs. Because I taught her to nurse herself to sleep, she became dependent on this and lost touch with her natural ability to go to sleep whenever she was tired.

EARLY LANGUAGE

I often try to imagine what it must be like, after months in the womb, to be able to see, hear, and touch the members of the family who one has already been listening to before birth. We observe that even a very young infant will stare closely at someone's face as they speak, appearing to connect the memory of this voice with the voice and face in the present moment.

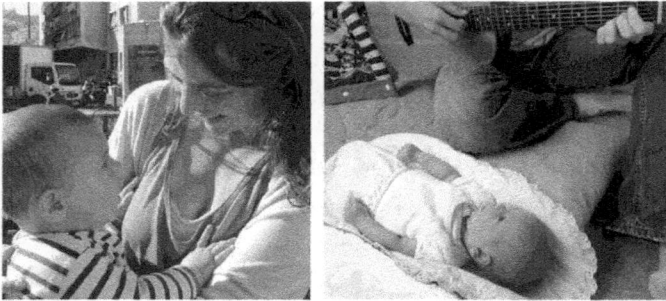

Another support of language development can be seen at this young age, the attempt to imitate facial expressions and mouth movements of the other person. Such exercise of the mouth in imitation is a vital stage of the development of language. Because of all this important language exploration that is going on, we try—whenever a child is watching, studying, our face—to never look away until he does, until he is finished with his studying of our face or voice; for this is his most important education in the moment.

Singing a song to an infant that he has heard before birth can be very calming. This is the time to share the song, the music, even the musical instruments, of a family and the wider community.

Motherese/Parentese

Motherese or parentese, is a way some people speak to a newborn with a high-pitched voice and simple sentences and is observed all over the world. It is an expression of adoration of a cute and helpless being, like the way we might speak to a new little kitten. It has its use for us adults when we spontaneously express our feelings when first meeting a new baby; but this has value only in the adult's first expression of welcome, not as a loving model of language.

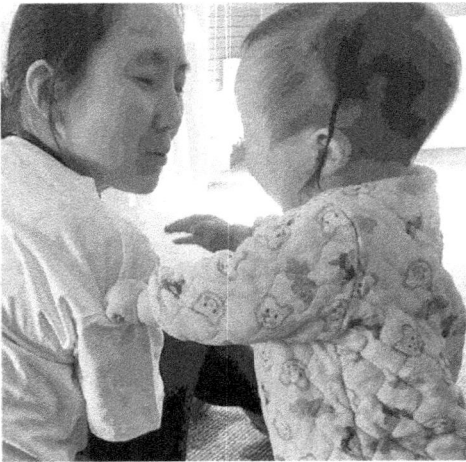

If we observe carefully, we will see that, even in these early months, an infant attempts to imitate our way of talking, and tries to communicate with us. Whenever we make eye-contact during the infant care activities of the day, such as changing a diaper or dressing, and try to imitate as closely as possible the attempts the child makes to communicate with us, we can truly engage in a conversation.

Even from these first days of life, family and friends are modeling language, so we must try to remember to use the best, most precise, language—and speak in the same tone of voice we would use with each other.

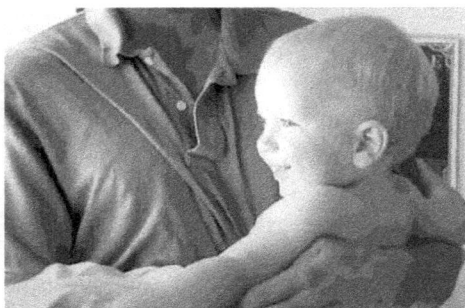

When our son, a musician, met his nephew for the first time he wanted to share his own joy of music. So, after looking through his sister's music CDs he played short clips of music of many different kinds. Holding the child in his arms he moved with him to the rhythm of the music that was being played. Clearly the infant's brain was making connections between the sounds and the movements, each piece of music, and the accompanying movement, clearly enjoyed. This little boy is now in high school and very talented in music.

From the early days, an infant is learning the details of the language of the family and community, the objects and actions; the volume and tone of voice; the sentence structure; the vocabulary; and the musicality because each language has its own "song." Clearly preparation for speaking, writing, and reading, begins now.

One of the ways to support this stage of education is to tell the child what you are doing, using the exact names and adjectives of objects:

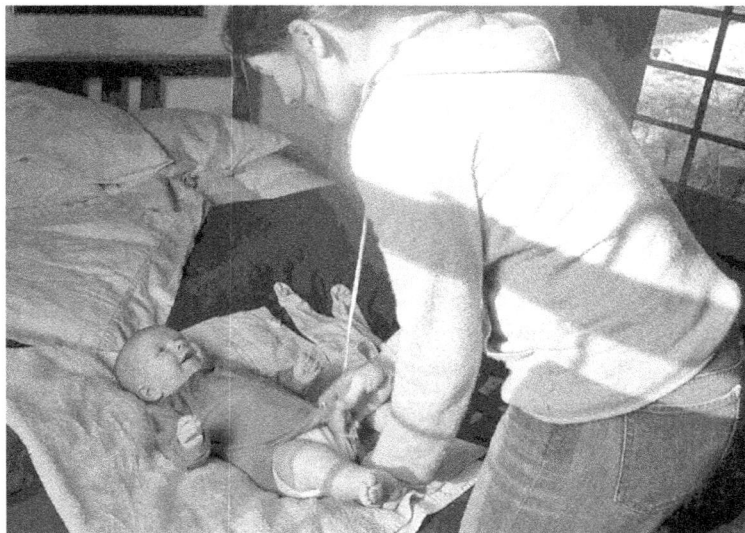

This is a soft, blue jumpsuit that I am putting on you. Now I am snapping the buttons. Now I am going to sing a "dressing" song to you that my parents sang to me when I was a baby. I hope you enjoy it.

MOVEMENT

The more free-movement and exploration and interaction with people and in the environment, the more a child will want, and be able to, express in language.

The director of my Montessori 0-3 training, Silvana Montanaro was an MD in the field of psychiatry, she told us that 50% of crying is eliminated by giving the infant the possibility of free movement.

Safety

As parents prepare for the child to join the family throughout the day, every bit of the room must be examined carefully to be sure that everything is safe to be touched by the infant—the floor, the lower walls, the furniture—because there are always unexpected leaps in physical ability when a child is allowed to move freely.

A father in Poland, who was using Montessori ideas at home with their new baby, sent me an amazing video of his son who was just learning to crawl.

The infant slept on a mattress on the bedroom floor and even though the door to the rest of the apartment was left open the parents carried him to the living room to be with them when they heard that he was awake.

One day he decided to make the trip on his own. He crawled to the edge of the mattress and rocked back and forth, sometimes reaching down to touch the floor, as if he was judging the exact movement necessary to get to the floor. Occasionally he looked up at the dad and smiled but it was clear he wanted to do this on his own.

Finally, slowly, he touched the floor with both hands, pulled himself onto the floor, and crawled into the living room to join the family.

To encourage movement and inspire learning, we can place some touchable items on a low shelf in every room or arrange them in such a way that they can safely be handled by a child who is just learning to crawl and sit up on his own. This will give pleasure and encourage to use the hand in new ways.

I once watched one of my grandchildren, who was exploring a shelf of bowls and other metal containers in our kitchen begin to match the size of a lid to different containers to see which would fit. This is an example of the development of the mathematical mind.

Hands free!

Sometime in the first year a child learns to move to a seated position on his own. There are many new activities that can be attempted now with hands free. And when there is a child-size table and chair available, the child can even begin to eat with a spoon and fork, pour himself a glass of water from a small pitcher, and serve himself food from a serving bowl. How satisfying this must feel to be able to work on the skills he has observed in the family for months.

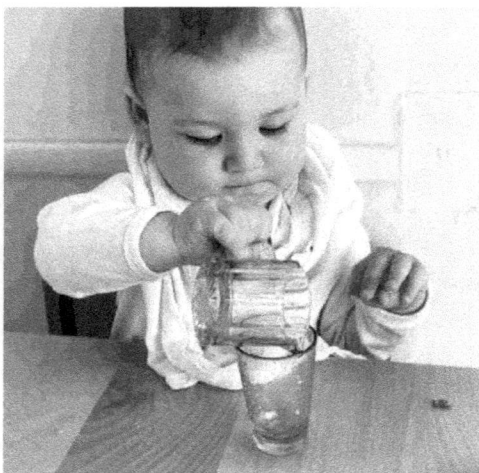

Montessori states over and over, in many ways, that there is a strong connection between the work of the hands and mental development. She points out that a child's intelligence, when helped by work with the hands, can reach a higher level and the character will be stronger.

Pulling up

The best situation for this practice is when a child can work on the new skill at any time, not dependent on someone else to pull him up.

Once I visited a family where there was a piano, clearly of interest to a child just learning to crawl. It was fascinating to watch the little girl pull herself up to the keys of the piano, play a note, carefully let herself down, and then repeat this cycle over and over.

It seemed as though the new movement challenge, and the music, were both calling her.

FIRST STEPS

The path to mastery of the stages of language and movement in the first year are unique to every child. It seems that they listen to themselves and then decide what to work on next:

Now I am going to spend my free-movement time to practice turning over, again and again and again. Oh, my mother is telling me the names of everything I can touch in the kitchen and that is just what I was interested in today. I am going to practice making the sounds I hear my family speak and sing all day. It seems that everyone around me is standing up and walking so today I am going to work on that. And so on.

It is very important not to compare one child with another, but to learn to observe and take joy in what he is working on right now, and to accept him exactly as he is, and respect what he has chosen to work on in this moment.

Then we can, without feelings of competition, enjoy what both our own child, and those of our friends, are working on at any one time.

The best situation is when a child is not rushed to learn to walk by being held— "helped"—by an adult holding him up to practice. If the adult patiently supports a child's individual mastery of crawling, pulling up, and standing, then taking those first steps on his own is an experience of great joy.

Once the human being has learned to stand and walk the possibilities of development grow exponentially. This child will be able to imitate even more of what he sees going on in the world of the home and close community and, with a lot of forethought and planning on the part of the adults, will be able to participate and even contribute to the well-being of the group.

FIRST WORDS

Along with movement changes by the end of the first year, language takes a great leap. We might not understand what the child is saying to us, but we can make eye-contact, turn off our phones, listen, and engage more and more in conversation.

At one year of age the child says his first intentional word . . . his babbling has a purpose, and this intention is a proof of conscious intelligence...He becomes ever more aware that language refers to his surroundings, and his wish to master it consciously becomes also greater . . . Subconsciously and unaided, he strains himself to learn, and this effort makes his success all the more astonishing.

—Montessori, *The Absorbent Mind*

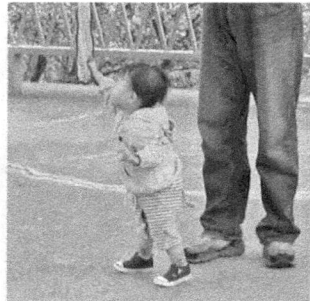

While in Japan I observed a father or grandfather showing his very young son or grandson around a temple. There was a giant metal bell that was struck by pulling back a heavy rope attached to a very long and thick log.

The adult showed the young boy how it worked and then the little one reached for the rope. The adult understood that he wanted to ring the bell, and so he handed it to the child and exerted just enough pull himself to ring the bell. The little boy left very satisfied with his success.

Exploring is natural, and giving exact language of these experiences allows the child to share what he is learning

Participating in the daily work of the family and community—activities with a clear purpose—has a natural consequence of the joy of being a valuable part of a group, even at this young age.

One of the discoveries Montessori made over one hundred years ago was that children would rather be doing the work that they see others carrying out, than play with toys. So, she began to have real tools created that were of good quality and a size that made the work more manageable by the young. Today we find items that were not available before: small tables and chairs, stools to reach the kitchen sink in the home, short-handled brooms and mops, even child-size wheelbarrows to haul soil and wood chips for the home garden.

Whenever one is carrying out a common activity at home, such as wrapping gifts, if a child wants to participate, one must learn to quickly analyze the steps involved and figure out which step will match the ability of the child who is watching and seems interested in joining us. One child will be able to smooth out the wrapping paper to be used, another is happy to hold down the gift as the adult ties the ribbon. As the child grows there will be more ways to participate in gift-wrapping, such as cutting the paper or ribbon, writing the gift tag, or tying the ribbon. This is a good example of the value of the adult learning to observe—discovering just where the child is at any given moment, because change is continual—and then figuring out what to offer.

The adult at home and in the Montessori infant community

Before going any further I would like to point out that the trained Montessori teacher for this age is skilled at observations of this kind. She has nothing to distract her as she goes about her day combining knowledge of Montessori theory and what she sees is needed by each individual child at any one moment.

Parents or grandparents, on the other hand, have many roles to fill during a day. If there is time to begin to use all the ideas in the book all the better, but if not, just take time to think and perhaps try one tiny change a week. It is common knowledge that each person is doing the very best for his or her child with the knowledge, the time, and the energy, in the moment.

Gardening and caring for animals

There is plenty of work that could be shared both at home and in the Montessori class. Some examples are gardening and caring for animals. They can be done with the adult in the home but are usually arranged for the child to do at any time in the infant community.

For example, after a lesson on picking cherry tomatoes there will be a garden basket available all day and any time during the day a child, who has learned to pick tomatoes carefully, can choose to do this work.

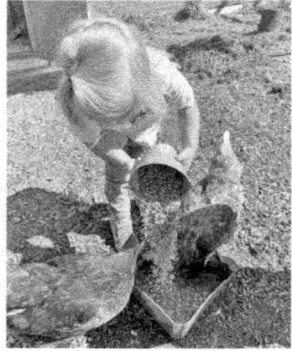

When feeding animals, the parent or teacher puts out the exact amount of food that the animal needs. In the infant community this usually means fish food to put in the aquarium, but in the home, it could also be for pets. Children quickly learn that when the day's food is out and ready anyone can feed the animal; and when the food is given to the animal, the work is done. The care and consideration of the animal is always the highest priority; an important lesson modeled for children.

Flower arranging

Flower arranging is a favorite activity in the home, the infant community and the Montessori primary class. The arrangement can be of whatever wild plants are blooming, flowers in the garden, or flowers brought into the environment by the adult, or even, when no flowers are available, a stem from a tree with leaves. The simple arrangements are often made of just one item that is placed in a small vase, given water, and then placed on the snack, lunch, or other table.

A friend once sent me a video of a young child doing the flower arranging work in an infant community. He was not yet a year and a half old and had been shown this work (given a lesson) by the teacher four months earlier.

A lesson in a Montessori class at all ages can be given 1:1 by the teacher, by another student, or even by carefully watching someone else doing the work. So, this child had clearly been watching and mastering some of the elements of the work—carrying items carefully, getting water in the bathroom, pouring water, placing objects carefully on a table, correcting mistakes such as doing the steps of a task out of order, and more.

It was clear that he was thinking deeply about each step, making errors and correcting himself, being aware of the order and logic of the work, being flexible, remembering steps, deciding on and reaching goals, and throughout the whole work he was calm, patient, confident, working without frustration. This was a wonderful example of executive functions that is way beyond commonly held belief in the capabilities of a child under the age of two years.

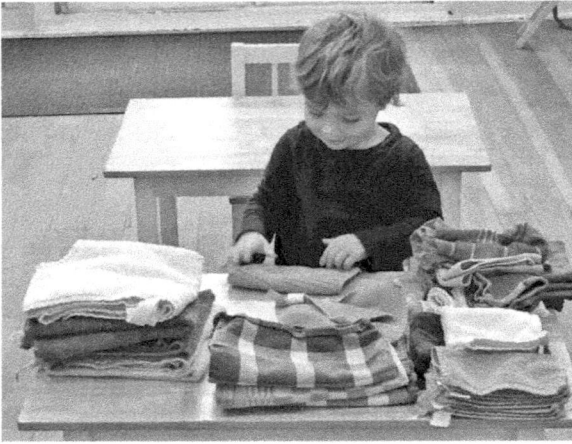

Folding cloths in the infant community is one of many of
the activities kept always ready and available on the shelf. But
some folding is only carried out occasionally. An example is
helping to put away the clean laundry. When a basket of
freshly washed polishing cloths, hand towels, and aprons has
been brought into the classroom it is placed on the floor near
the area where these items are kept. Any child can then
approach the work, remove one piece at a time from the
laundry basket, place it on a table and fold it, sort it into piles,
and then put everything away. Folding is a favorite activity
and something that can be done at home.

Meals

Almost anything having to do with food is interesting at this age: planting and harvesting vegetables, cutting fruit, peeling eggs, arranging food on plates, setting the table, serving food, cleaning up after a snack or meal by washing and drying the table, sweeping the floor, mopping, and even washing the dishes.

Observing in a Montessori infant community I watched a very young child who was setting the table for lunch for the first time. He and the teacher each held a two-handle basket that was placed on the shelf. The teacher, and then the child, each placed only one plate in each of their baskets. Then, over and over, carried the plates one at a time to the lunch table, carefully putting them on the table above where each chair was placed. When the plates were all set in place, they did the same with glasses, one at a time. And then spoons and forks.

The teacher only collaborated until it was clear, with each new stage, that the child knew what to do, then she turned to something else, keeping her eye on him to be ready to show him the next step.

This kind of repetition, combining the work of the body (learning to walk while carrying something), the hands, and the brain, is a perfect example of real learning. It is also an early example of feeling useful and helping friends in the community.

How to begin to offer real work in the home

Figuring out how to include the child in the work of the family in the home is very different than in a classroom. The home environment is used by everyone at any age, and most work must usually be done efficiently and quickly, because there is so much to do in a modern home today. But there is usually a way.

We can start with one item, for example a floor broom with the long handle cut to a length so that a young child can use it—if a child-sized broom is not available. Prepare the broom and then decide on the most logical place to keep it. Fasten a short cord to the end, attached a hook to the wall, and show the child where the broom should be hung when it is not being used.

Just as in the classroom, in the beginning, the child will forget to hang the broom up when he is finished. In the classroom it might be another child who notices and puts the broom away, or the teacher, and gradually the child remembers that putting the work away is part of the work cycle and does it for himself. In the home a sibling or adult can also use this broom to sweep, and then put it away, modeling for the child who will eventually learn to do it.

Then perhaps think of the next task to prepare for the child's participation. The important thing is to observe the child's face as we carry out our daily work. If there is an interest, offer a way to participate. If it is possible for a child to choose a task at any time—for example setting a table which could be done at any time of the day—show the steps so the child can manage on his own. If not, joyfully work together.

Why does the interest in a task wane?

It is typical from this age through the primary class age of 6.5 years, that a child will master a task and then stop being interested. Even though we might expect that once a child, for example, learns to cut and arrange flowers to decorate the home or classroom, he will continue to do this. But this is not what happens.

The child at this age is working—from an interior guide— to master a task or skill. Then he moves on to the next challenge. We say that this child is not creating the environment, he is creating himself.

LANGUAGE

Language – vocabulary

All examples of work a child can carry out in the home and classroom, that were shared in this chapter, are enriched by learning the names of the objects and actions involved. With this vocabulary a child can explain what he wants to do, share his experiences, have more to talk about with his family. And each time a new word is learned, the connections in the brain are made more secure and important education has taken place.

Walking on the beach at low tide one day, with my two-year-old granddaughter, I pointed out the *bull kelp seaweed*, the *ochre sea star* (starfish), the *California mussels*, and the *green anemone* and invited her to touch these things. Then I gave her the name. Over and over, she touched and named, touched and named, and when we returned home told her parents about these creatures using the correct name. They were thrilled at her excitement about sharing her trip to the beach and astonished with her vocabulary. But these new words are no more difficult than the names of fruit and vegetables and clothing and cars, etc., and learning the vocabulary enabled her to tell her parents about the day.

Books

At this age vocabulary books are of great interest to the child, especially when they contain pictures of items he has seen in the home and community such as clothing, tools, farm animals, kitchen objects, etc. Look for pictures, if possible, with a white background behind the object being named, to avoid confusion. For example, if the bird is perched on a branch of a tree surrounded by leaves, exactly what is the parent pointing to when giving the name "robin?" Learning these words can increase the child's desire and ability to speak.

Listening, the gift of our attention

Even more valuable than modeling correct language and giving rich vocabulary, is the gift of our time and attention. It takes just a moment or two to halt the preparation of the meal, to bend down or sit so that our face is at a level as the child's face and make eye contact, when he starts to tell us something. Many families have a no-phone rule at meals and sometimes in front of young children. All Montessori schools that I know of have a no-phone rule during the school day.

We adults are used to cell-phone interruption when we are with friends, but it is very difficult for a child at a young age to understand. The clear message is that for some reason, a small object has taken his parent away and he doesn't understand why.

MUSIC

Music is so valuable that it should be modeled for the young before birth and then every day throughout life. Often, we adults most easily remember the songs we learned at a certain age, and sometimes they will even inspire us to dance. What an example for children in the home when we share music and dance that we love.

In a Montessori infant community, I watched a two-year-old spend a lot of time in the music area of the infant community. She laid out a small rug next to the music shelves, placed a container of musical instruments pictures on the rug, slowly look through them, and returned them to the shelf. Then, one at a time, she moved other items to the rug and explored them: playing each of the percussion instruments in a basket, and a small xylophone. After putting everything away, including the rug, she started singing a song and acting it out, "knees and shoulders, heads and toes."

This is a typical example of individual choice of work in Montessori classes. A child might have been introduced to songs in a small, spontaneously formed group activity with the adult, but singing goes on at any time of the day, as does all the other work.

Musical instruments

There is so much recorded music available today that it is quite common for a young child to have no idea that it is the movement of the human body that creates music. Whenever possible try to show a child a real musical instrument. If a relative or friend plays an instrument, ask him or her to demonstrate it.

A child can be shown how to touch it carefully, sometimes even playing it. One child might be interested in learning the name of the instrument, and another the name and maybe even the names of the parts of the instrument; another child might be interested in the names of the notes played and the songs that are played. Follow the child.

PRAISE

When the child completes the work, we are very careful not to praise. We accept effort and work as normal for any member of the family or community. Most of all, rather than being in charge of what the child does, we try to protect the connection between the uniquely developing child and his own inner guide to choose work intelligently, concentrate, and create balance and happiness through his efforts.

Excessive praise can disrupt a child's concentration and even destroy his own intrinsic motivation for carrying out an activity, such as working hard or helping someone.

Working for the approval or praise of the parent or teacher can break the connection with the wise internal drive, making a child more focused on external validation. This can prevent learning and halt the development of independent thinking and responsible action.

It is best, when we are sure it will not interrupt concentration, to just acknowledge effort, exactly as we might do with a friend who is pitching in to help, acknowledging effort without judgmental praise.

CONCENTRATION

Over and over in Montessori theory and practice we hear about the value of concentration. Once a child has begun the work and is concentrating, we step back and protect the concentration, because deep concentration is a healing in many ways, at every stage and age of Montessori learning. As Montessori tells us, we must carefully work out an environment that would present the most favorable external conditions for this concentration.

One of the most important results of Montessori practice, confirmed for over 100 years all over the world, is that the kindness, compassion, and a desire to help others, is an inborn characteristic of the human being. It appears following concentration. Not concentration on scrolling on a phone for example, but concentration that aligns with the stage of development of the individual, has been self-chosen, involves the mind and body working together toward an intelligent purpose, and that is protected from interruption until a personally set goal is attained.

Understanding the value of concentration can inspire us to look around the home or classroom, to carefully study the impulses of our child, and learn to figure out how to provide important work for a child and then get out of the way.

What better foundation for becoming a happy, confident, creative, and compassionate human being could there be?

In each of my talks over the years, and in most of my books I share the following quote:

When the children had completed an absorbing bit of work, they appeared rested and deeply pleased . . . as if a road had opened up within their souls that led to all their latent powers, revealing the better part of themselves.

They . . . put themselves out to help others and seemed full of good will.

Thereafter, I set out to find experimental objects that would make this concentration possible, and carefully worked out an environment that would present the most favorable external conditions for this concentration.

And that is how my method began.

—Montessori, *The Child in the Family*

THE AUTHOR

My first discoveries of the many ways people live and are educated, began during the 1963-1964 trip mentioned in the introduction to this book. What I observed around the world lit a fire of curiosity that is still burning. I returned home to discover that so many situations that we consider universal are not inborn; they are caused by society's expectations and treatment of children.

For example, *the terrible twos* or the *teenage problem*; these modern problems do not exist in some places; they are not genetic. They are a result of lack of understanding of, and providing for, the needs of two extremely creative, and independence-searching periods of life, ages 0-6 and ages 12-18. And when students at the 6-12 age are allowed to fulfill their needs to form groups, to work together and support each other rather than competing, and to follow their own curiosity to an ever-widening field of research and learning, it is not necessary to use rewards for them to learn a great deal. And when they learn joyfully the skills and information will be remembered.

Over the years I have continued to learn from my own family and friends, from my students between the ages of two and eighteen and their parents. I have learned from college professors in several universities, earning degrees in philosophy, world religions, and education, including a class at the Harvard Graduate School of Education led by Howard Gardner of multiple intelligences fame.

When our teenage daughters, inspired by the birth of their new baby brother, started a little store and named it after the baby, "The Michael Olaf Montessori Store," I was able to answer questions about child development from customers, parents and teachers of all kinds. Soon we were invited to exhibit our books and materials at conferences around the US and beyond, where I learned even more about the needs of parents and teachers in our modern world.

I began recording these conversations in the pages of the Michael Olaf catalogues, and eventually in books like that one you are reading.

I feel blessed that my books are appreciated by a broad audience. My own curiosity and broad experience explains the reason: I traveled to Italy to visit the Reggio Emilia program; attended lectures at the Suzuki education center in Matsumoto, Japan which inspired me to study Suzuki viola and piano; visited Waldorf schools in the UK and the US; earned three AMI (Association Montessori Internationale) diplomas; gave workshops to teachers of the California HeadStart program; spent many years as an administrator and teacher in Montessori schools; tutored high school Latin; worked as a counselor for girls in a detention center; homeschooled our last child for twelve years.

Completely unexpectedly, I have been able to help adults working in orphanages in Morocco and Colombia, teachers at TCV, the Tibetan Children's Village in India, and to advise on education for several governments and speak in teacher-education classes in several universities. Today I work as a consultant, speaker, and examiner for Montessori teacher courses, a writer excited to continue to share what I continue to learn, and as an artist sharing some of the paintings on the covers of my books.

Hopefully what you find in the pages of this book will help in your own search for joy and purpose.

BOOKS IN THIS SERIES

*(*) = books in this series containing information
on the first three years*

(*) *Aid to Life, Montessori Beyond the Classroom*

An experience of teaching "Montessori" in a private girls' school in Peru with no Montessori materials; a newspaper column; homeschooling experiences for age 6-19; Montessori help in Nepal, Tibet, Sikkim, Russia, Morocco: EsF (Educateurs sans Frontieres) Thailand: ideas for the home for ages 0-18; a grandparenting literary experience; observation of a typical day in a Montessori primary class (age 2.5-6.5) in London.

(*) *Beginnings, Montessori Birth to Three Comparison with Traditions in Bhutan*

Welcomed by new parents-to-be who are overwhelmed by parenting advice because here they can compare two well-tested parenting methods and decide what aligns with their own hopes.

Child of the World:
Montessori, Global Education for Age 3-12+

A brief overview of theory and practice in the Montessori primary, age 2.5-6.5 classroom. The same for the elementary class for ages 6-12. Other chapters: stages of development; the young adult; the adult; preparing the environment; parenting and teaching

Glimpses of Aged Care through a Montessori Lens

Created by Anne Kelly, head of the AMI Montessori for Dementia, Disability, and Ageing training program, and Susan

Mayclin Stephenson. They share their unique and complimentary experiences and attitudes toward the last stage of life. This book is enlightening and helpful in cultures where discussions of old age and death are avoided and, as a result, there is little or no preparation.

(*) *Montessori and Mindfulness*

When practiced authentically, Montessori students spend most of the day being mindful and in the moment. External mindful practices, valuable in other situations, would get in the way. Chapters include: support and impediments of mindfulness; flow; mindful work, walking, music, exploration; born to be good, and a chapter on mindfulness contributed by the psychologist Dr. Angeline Lillard.

(*) *Montessori Cosmic Education,*
The Child's Discovery of a Global Vision
and a Cosmic Task

A brief introduction to a main Montessori education purpose, which is learning about the world and the interconnectedness of all life, and the search for, and discovery of, one's unique contribution to the world. Ideas for birth through 6-12 years of age are presented.

(*) *Montessori for Family and Community*

Ideas for using tested practices to support the optimum development of children and young adults from birth through the high school or secondary years in such a way that they will get in touch with their own authentic self, learn in enjoyable, and become adults that will contribute to a better world.

Because of many requests, this book will be made available in four smaller booklets, for ages 0-3, 3-6, 6-12, and 12-18.

(*) ***Joy and Purpose, the Infant-Toddler Years***
Joy and Purpose, the Preschool Years
Joy and Purpose, the School Years
Joy and Purpose, the Teenage Years

Montessori Homeschooling

This documentation of a homeschool experiment through elementary, middle, and high school is an inspiration to parents and teachers with only traditional education experience who hope for something more practical, enjoyable, and successful for their children and students.

No Checkmate, Montessori Chess lessons for Age 3-90+

A Montessori way of teaching chess is just one example of how to follow a child's interest and stage of development when teaching any skill. Examples are grace and courtesy of handling the chess pieces; social aspect of the game; practical life— polishing/dusting the pieces, setting up the environment; language, using the three-period-lesson to learn the names of the pieces; mastering the game by building up one difficulty at a time. It is based on the author's years of teaching chess to young children.

Please Help Me Do It Myself, Observation and Recordkeeping for the Primary and Elementary Class

Montessori practice requires a scientist's ability to observe carefully, record observations, think, make an individual plan for each child, and act on this plan—and then continue to observe and adapt depending on the child's choices and mastery. At the 6-12 level the author shares how her students themselves mastered record keeping, planning, learning to make and meet goals (including local state/country requirements) and manage time. Additional primary class chapters: general knowledge book of the teacher; formal language book; beginning a new class; first six weeks in a continuing class; moving to a new environment; parent communication; human needs and tendencies; becoming a young adult.

(*) *The Joyful Child: Montessori,*
Global Wisdom for Birth to Three

Five chapters with information and support for development in the first years of life; ten chapters on the development in the second two years. Also, preparing the environment; parenting and teaching; the Montessori approach to weaning; the Montessori 0-3 or Assistants to Infancy parent/teacher training.

This is the most translated book of this series and has brought Montessori to parents in many places.

(*) *The Music Environment for All Ages,*
Montessori Foundations for the Creative Personality

A version of this information was joint published by AMI (Association Montessori Internationale) and NAMTA (North American Montessori Teachers Association) in the AMI Journal 2014-2015 issue: *The Montessori Foundations for the Creative Personality*. It gives parents and other educators an overview of the value and practice of music in the different stages of life: 0-3, 3-6, 6-12, 12-18, and even for the elderly.

The Red Corolla, Montessori Cosmic Education
(for age 3-6+)

Chapters include cosmic education; the work of the adult; the work of the child; culture from birth to age twelve; the music environment; and a Montessori glossary. There are universally tested cultural activities for this age: physics, botany, zoology, history, geography, art, music. In each area there is specific practical life work, sensorial exploration, lessons, sometimes artwork, and always the language that follows the experiences. All this information is based on lectures delivered in an AMI primary diploma course by the author.

(*) *The Universal Child, Guided by Nature*

(Part 1) Natural, inborn, human tendencies on which Montessori at all ages is based: movement, work, maximum effort, perfection, concentration, self-control, belonging, communication, and joy.

(Part 2) Sharing Montessori in a variety of cultures.

(Part 3) and the needs of adults whether they have, or have not, been met in the early formative years.

(Part 4) How closeness to nature aids human development.

Joy and Purpose, the Infant-Toddler Years

Copyright © 2025 Susan Mayclin Stephenson

Book 1 in the *Montessori for Family and Community* series
Adapted from the book *Montessori for Family and Community*

Cover: from a painting by the author of a child exploring his home

Michael Olaf Montessori Company
PO Box 1162
Arcata, CA 95518, USA
www.michaelolaf.net
michaelolafcompany@gmail.com
ISBN 978-1-879264-39-7

Translation and foreign publishing rights
contact: michaelolafbooks@gmail.com

More Montessori Information
https://susanart.net
www.montessori.edu
www.michaelolaf.net
https://susanmayclinstephenson.net

Adult/child references: to avoid confusion, "she" usually refers to an adult and "he" to a child.

Reprint Permission: Permission is granted to share quotes from the book in newsletters, blogs, articles, university papers, books, book reviews, or via the Internet—if it is being shared without requesting payment, and if it includes a clear reference to this title, and the full name of the author.

Gratitude for pictures and video clips: I am grateful to the parents and teachers from around the world who have allowed me to record, through photos and video, children's stages of development to help others understand more deeply.

QR codes: The video clips on our YouTube collection, "Montessori for family and community" can be accessed via the QR codes on the pages of this book and at the QR code below.

Please feel free to share them with anyone who will benefit.

OBSERVATION NOTES:

OBSERVATION NOTES:

www.ingramcontent.com/pod-product-compliance
Lightning Source LLC
Chambersburg PA
CBHW022344040426
42449CB00006B/708